Take Care of Yourself

Caring for Your Teeth

Siân Smith

Heinemann
LIBRARY

Chicago, Illinois

www.capstonepub.com
Visit our website to find out
more information about
Heinemann-Raintree books.

To order:

☎ Phone 800-747-4992

🖥 Visit www.capstonepub.com
to browse our catalog and order online.

Edited by Dan Nunn, Rebecca Rissman,
   and John-Paul Wilkins
Designed by Victoria Allen
Picture research by Tracy Cummins
Production by Alison Parsons
Originated by Capstone Global Library Ltd
Printed and bound in China by Leo Paper Products Ltd

16 15 14 13 12
10 9 8 7 6 5 4 3 2 1

Library of Congress Cataloging-in-Publication Data
Smith, Siân.
   Caring for your teeth / Siân Smith.
      p. cm.—(Take care of yourself!)
   Includes bibliographical references and index.
   ISBN 978-1-4329-6708-6 (hb)—ISBN 978-1-4329-6715-4 (pb)
1. Teeth—Care and hygiene—Juvenile literature. I. Title.
   RK63.S65 2013
   617.6—dc23   2011049837

Acknowledgments
We would like to thank the following for permission to
reproduce photographs: Capstone Library pp. 9, 12, 13, 23c
(Karon Dubke); Getty Images pp. 7 (Marilyn Conway), 8
(Peter Cade), 14 right (Tom Grill), 17, 20, 23a (Image Source),
19 (ERproductions Ltd), 22 (Tom Grill); istockphoto pp. 14 left
(© Kim Gunkel), 21 (© Richard Hydren); Shutterstock pp. 4
(© Vladimir Wrangel), 5 (© Monkey Business Images), 6, 23b
(© Levent Konuk), 10 (© Gemenacom), 11 (© ilFede), 15
(© Alexander Trinitatov), 146 (© Jaimie Duplass), 18
(© Andreas Gradin).

Front cover photograph of girl brushing her teeth
reproduced with permission of Getty Images (Blend
Images). Rear cover photograph of funny young girl
eating corn reproduced with permission of Shutterstock
(© ladimir Wrangel).

Every effort has been made to contact copyright holders
of material reproduced in this book. Any omissions will be
rectified in subsequent printings if notice is given to the
publisher.

We would like to thank Nesha Patel, Nancy Harris, and Dee
Reid for their assistance in the preparation of this book.

Contents

Why Should I Care for My Teeth?

You need your teeth to eat food.

Your teeth get plaque on them
after you eat.

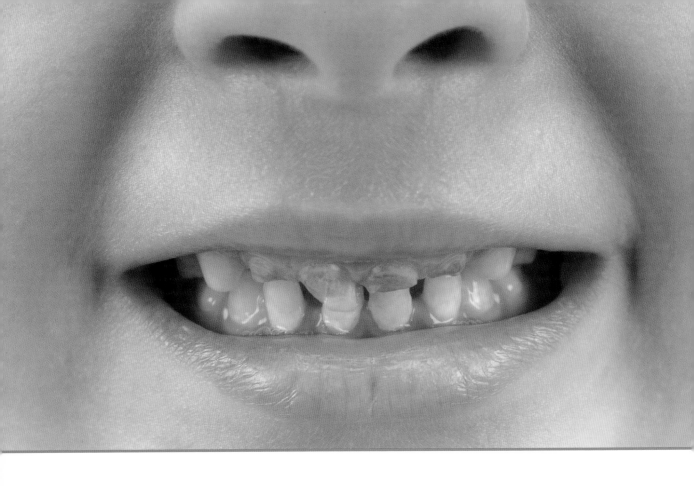

Plaque makes teeth rot.

This makes your teeth hurt.

How to Brush Your Teeth

When you brush your teeth,
you get rid of the plaque.

Put a pea-sized bit of toothpaste
on your brush.

Brush around every tooth.

Brush the places that are hard to reach, too.

timer

Brush for about two minutes.
You could use a timer to help you.

Spit the toothpaste out in the sink.

When Should I Brush My Teeth?

Brush your teeth after breakfast.

Brush your teeth before you sleep.

Brush your teeth after lunch
or snacks if you can.

Other Ways to Care for Your Teeth

You can drink water at any time.
Water is not bad for your teeth.

Candy is bad for your teeth.
Sugary drinks are bad for your teeth.

17

Try not to have sweet things
very often.

Brush your teeth afterward
if you can.

You should see the dentist
twice a year.

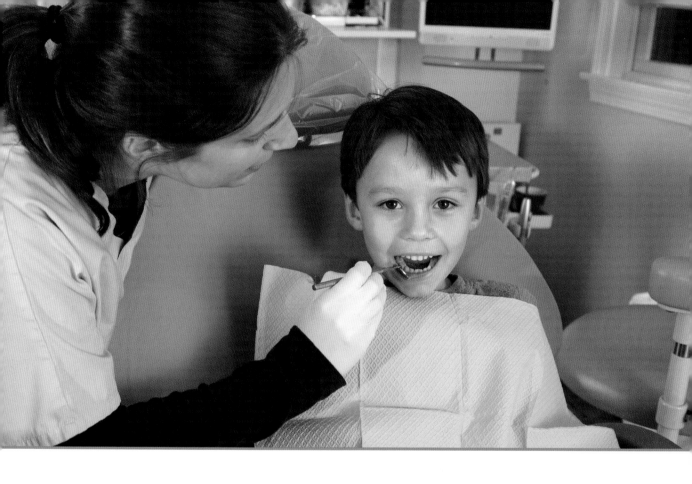

The dentist will check to see if your
teeth are clean and healthy.

Can You Remember?

When should you brush your teeth?

Answer on page 24

Picture Glossary

dentist doctor who looks after people's teeth

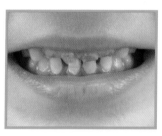

plaque something you get on your teeth after you eat or drink. You cannot see plaque, but it is bad for your teeth.

timer machine a bit like a clock. A timer can tell you how long it takes to do something.

Index

Answer to question on page 22
You need to brush your teeth after breakfast and before you go to bed.
You should also brush your teeth after eating lunch, snacks, or sweet things if you can.

Notes for parents and teachers
Before reading
Ask the children why we need teeth. Find out what they know about how to take care of their teeth and record their ideas. Read the book to see where these ideas overlap.

After reading
- If possible, ask a dentist or hygienist to speak to the children about what they need to do to take care of their teeth. Use a toothbrush, model of teeth, and a timer and ask a child to brush the teeth for 2 minutes. Which teeth were harder to clean? Demonstrate how to brush your teeth well.

- Draw a face with an open, smiling mouth (crescent shaped). Give the children a quiz on how to care for their teeth. For each question they get right, add a tooth to the mouth. Can they collect a full set of teeth?